MUM
RECIPES

Produced for
Malawi Underprivileged Mums

by
Linda McDonald RGN, RM

Published by **Linda McDonald**

ISBN Nº: 0-9551690-0-3

Front cover & illustrations drawn by **Sally McDonald**

Designed & printed by **Smart Design & Print Ltd**
www.smartdesignandprint.com

CONTENTS

INTRODUCTION

Malawi Underprivileged Mums is a registered charity which was set up earlier this year, after a team from Simpson Maternity Centre in The Royal Infirmary of Edinburgh visited Bottom Hospital, Lilongwe, Malawi. Bottom Hospital got its name when affluent people built a hospital nearby called Top Hospital, leaving the poorer people to the worse institution.

Bottom was, without doubt, the most deprived hospital seen by the Simpson's team. The conditions were appalling. Those who work there struggle with a lack of staff, a lack of basic equipment and poor infection control. Many of the women in the region live in rural villages far from the hospital and have no transport when they go into labour. This, combined with the poor state of the hospital itself, has resulted in very high maternal and infant death rates.

Last year alone, 58 mothers died in Bottom Hospital and there were 22 stillbirths per thousand births—the hospital having around 11,500 deliveries per year. The maternal death rate in Malawi is approximately 1:29 compared to 1:8000 in the United Kingdom. Malawi has one of the worst, if not the worst, mortality rates in the world.

Many of the mother and infant deaths can be prevented through better education, equipment and transport. MUMs hopes to make a substantial difference to the lives of the mothers and babies of Bottom Hospital.

THE BUTTERFLY

The butterfly was the Simpson Memorial Maternity Pavilion hospital badge. It was presented to a newly qualified midwife on completion of her training in the hospital. Sir James Young Simpson discovered anaesthesia and was the first doctor to apply a modern anaesthetic, ether, to alleviate the pain of labour. The butterfly comes from the tombstone of Sir James, buried in Warriston Cemetery, Edinburgh, and the inscription *Victo Dolore* (pain conquered) is on his coat of arms.

The butterfly symbolises, beauty, metamorphosis and the human spirit. In Japan, the butterfly is the symbol for young womanhood.

Although the badge is no longer issued, the butterfly logo is used throughout the Simpson Centre for Reproductive Health.

FOREWORD

I come from a family where social life and food are intimately connected. In an age in which there are so many distractions, our families happily still eat around the table. I have never known it any other way. I still have very clear memories as a small girl of my grandmother in Ireland setting the table with napkins and silver napkin rings. She was a stickler for manners and table etiquette; something she has passed on to me.

From these early beginnings, while watching my mother and grandmother in the kitchen, I developed a strong and abiding interest in food. Not just in the social occasions but in what was served there—in the recipes themselves. I'm always in hot pursuit of successful new dishes. Whenever I'm out in a restaurant or at friends', if there is something I particularly enjoy, I ask for the recipe or adapt it myself. I also collect recipes from magazines—it's always the first page I turn to—and I'm still using my mother's and grandmother's reliable favourites.

My recipes have been kept, like a lot of people's, in a jumbled mess in a file with an elastic band. Now, I've two reasons for bringing them together. My daughters are on the point of leaving home. Both they and I are aware of the need to pass on to them the recipes collected here. I hope they'll act as a survival kit, for there are quick dishes here and comfort food, as well as dishes for more sophisticated dining. But perhaps more importantly, this is a book of memories, a culinary photo album of all the family occasions we have shared.

For these reasons this book, in the most intimate sense, is for my family—in particular, for Katie and Sally. They've always been my best critics and biggest fans and so, in many ways, they have shaped this book. However, although it has always been in my mind to draw together these family recipes for Katie and Sally, I wouldn't have done it now without the trigger of the Simpson Maternity Centre's involvement with Bottom Hospital in Malawi. I can think of no better reason for sharing these recipes with you.

Linda McDonald
Edinburgh
October 2005

THE PELICAN

The Pelican was the Royal Infirmary of Edinburgh's hospital badge – now no longer issued. It was presented to a nurse who trained in the hospital and worked for a year after qualifying. This powerful image of maternal sacrifice depicts a mother pelican feeding her own flesh to her young.

ACKNOWLEDGEMENTS

I would like to thank and acknowledge the financial support of The Royal Bank of Scotland—whose generous investment turned a small idea into a much larger and more profitable concern. Thanks also to The Royal Infirmary of Edinburgh, The Simpson Centre for Reproductive Health, Lothian Health Board and the Pelican League who were hugely supportive from the outset.

I would like to thank Avoca, a fabulous Dublin restaurant, for allowing me to use some of the recipes from its book and to Stobo Castle, Health Spa, for its special dessert.

I would like to acknowledge the generous contributions of the following, without whose help this project would never have been realised:

- Graeme Walker and Anne Findlay who brought an awareness of the needs of Bottom Hospital to Edinburgh and who have given me so much support and encouragement
- Tom Pow, my wonderful brother-in-law, for casting his professional eye over the book
- Sarah and Barbara Watt and Laura Thornton for their individual expertise in typing and proof reading
- My daughter Sally for her beautiful art work.

My thanks also to Smart Design and Print for taking the work through to production and distribution—and for making my job so much easier—and to Alan and Jackie of Rankin Photography.

Special thanks to Lorna Pascall—without her by my side, checking recipes, teaching me computer skills with enormous patience and supporting my enthusiasm, this venture would have been beyond me and wouldn't have been half the fun.

I especially want to thank all my family, friends and colleagues who, over the last 25 years, have contributed to and shared in my love of cooking.

And finally, my deepest thanks to Iain, Katie and Sally, for their loyalty, support and love.

For my daughters, Katie and Sally

A KITCHEN PRAYER

Bless my little kitchen, Lord,
I love its every nook,
And bless me as I do my work,
Wash pots and clean and cook.

May the meals that I prepare
Be seasoned from above,
With Thy blessing and Thy grace,
But most of all Thy love.

As we partake of earthly food,
The table Thou hast spread,
We'll not forget to thank Thee Lord,
For all our daily bread.

So bless my little kitchen, Lord,
And those who enter in,
May they find naught but joy and peace,
And happiness therein.

AMEN

Anon

STARTERS

CHICKEN LIVER PÂTÉ

(Serves approx 8)

Otherwise known as Mum's Pâté (i.e. my Mum). A family favourite since school days, my school friends loved it too. Always asked as a contribution for Christmas and holidays and much nicer when Mum makes it!

Ingredients:

450g/1lb chicken livers, chopped, preferably fresh
1 medium sized onion, chopped
garlic to taste, at least 2 cloves
140ml/ ¼ pint sherry
225g/ ½ lb butter
2 tbsp tomato purée
pinch tarragon and marjoram
1 bay leaf
salt and pepper

Method:

1. Sauté the onion and garlic in butter for 2-3 minutes without colouring.
2. Add chicken livers, tomato purée, herbs and seasonings.
3. Simmer for 35 minutes. Remove bay leaf.
4. Add sherry, liquidise and chill.
   Freezes well.

MUSHROOM PÂTÉ

(Serves 6)

Quick, easy and different, ideal for vegetarians. I have had this recipe for years and can't remember where I got it. This applies to many recipes as you go through the book.

Ingredients:

150g/5oz butter
225g/8oz mushrooms, chopped
1 small onion, chopped
25g/1oz fresh white breadcrumbs
110g/4oz Philadelphia cheese
1 tsp lemon juice
pinch nutmeg
salt and pepper

Method:

1. Melt butter in pan.
2. Add onion and mushrooms. Cook for 10 minutes.
3. Add remaining ingredients and liquidise.
4. Chill.

SMOKED MACKEREL PÂTÉ

(Serves 6)

Given to me when I was a student nurse, by a district nurse in the late 70's.

Ingredients:

225g/8oz smoked mackerel
3 tbsp horseradish sauce
grated rind of ½ lemon
3 tbsp double cream
25g/1oz softened butter
chopped parsley
salt and pepper

Method:

1. Combine all ingredients in a liquidiser and blend until pâté consistency.
2. Chill.

SALMON AND SMOKED TROUT TERRINE - *AVOCA*

(Serves 12-18)

This is fabulous for Christmas and big dinner parties. I use an electric carver to achieve a neat thin slice. It can be made a couple of days ahead and freezes easily.

Ingredients:

Juice of 1½ lemons
2 rounded tsp powdered gelatine
800g/1lb 12oz salmon fillet, cooked and flaked
110g/4oz smoked trout fillet, flaked
300ml/ ½ pint mayonnaise
300ml/ ½ pint double cream, lightly whipped
3 tsp horseradish sauce
1 bunch dill, chopped
200g/7oz sliced smoked salmon

Method:

1. Place the lemon juice in a bowl, sprinkle the gelatine on top and leave to sponge for 5 minutes.
2. Place the cooked salmon and smoked trout in a bowl and fold in the mayonnaise, cream and horseradish. Season well and stir in the chopped dill.
3. Line a 900g/2lb loaf tin with cling film. A good trick is to wet the tin first so that the cling film sticks to it. Line with slices of smoked salmon allowing a good overlap at the top.
4. Stand the bowl of gelatine in a small pan of simmering water and heat gently, without stirring, until melted.
5. Add some of the salmon mixture to the warm gelatine and then fold the gelatine thoroughly into the rest of the salmon mixture. Check the seasoning and pour mixture into the lined tin. Fold overlapping smoked salmon on top. Cover with cling film and chill overnight.

AUNTIE SHEILA' S SOUP

(Serves 8)

This recipe came from my mother's college friend and bridesmaid. Very popular with my girls.

Ingredients:

50g/2oz butter
1 onion, chopped
1 clove garlic, crushed
2 carrots, diced
2 potatoes, diced
400g can chopped tomatoes
225g/ ½ lb lentils, washed
1750ml/3 pints vegetable stock (I use cubes)
salt and pepper

Method:

1. Sauté onion and garlic for a few minutes in butter.
2. Add remaining ingredients.
3. Simmer for 30 minutes, stirring occasionally.

CREAM OF CARROT SOUP

(Serves 8)

This is a lovely soup and the quantities serve a good number. My mum's recipe.

Ingredients:

900g/2lb carrots, peeled and chopped roughly
350g/ ¾ lb onions chopped
50g/2oz butter
1750ml/3 pints chicken stock
¾ tsp curry powder
150g/5oz carton single cream
½ small tin (170g) evaporated milk
salt and pepper

Method:

1. Sauté onions and carrots in butter for 5-10 minutes.
2. Add stock and simmer for 1 hour.
3. Add salt and pepper to taste.
4. Liquidise, add curry, cream and evaporated milk.

CREAM OF MUSHROOM SOUP

(Serves 6)

Made frequently over the last 30 years. Very easy to double up and make large quantities.

Ingredients:

450g/1lb mushrooms, chopped (large open mushrooms have a better flavour and colour)
1 onion, chopped
900ml/1½ pints chicken stock
600ml/1 pint milk - full cream is best
110g/4oz butter
50g/2oz plain flour
2 dessert spoons soya sauce
salt and pepper

Method:

1. Melt 50g/2oz butter and sauté onion for a few minutes.
2. Add mushrooms and stock, cook gently for 10 minutes with lid on.
3. To make roux melt remaining 50g/2oz butter in a small pan then add flour and cook for a couple of minutes.
4. Put roux in liquidiser with milk, soya sauce and mushroom mixture.
5. Blend, reheat and season to taste.

Freezes well.

CREAM OF CARROT AND CORIANDER SOUP

(Serves 8)

First had this at Moira's house for lunch—it was yummy! Moira is a great friend and loves food almost as much as I do. Many recipes I use were once hers.

Ingredients:

75g/3oz butter
700g/1½ lb sliced carrots
225g/8oz onions, sliced
3 tbsp plain flour
1200ml/2 pints chicken stock
1 tbsp lemon juice
150g/5oz single cream
300ml-600ml/ ½ -1 pint milk
2 tbsp fresh coriander
bay leaf
salt and pepper

Method:

1. Sauté onions and carrots in butter for 5 minutes.
2. Add flour then gradually add stock, coriander and bay leaf.
3. Simmer for 20 minutes, remove bay leaf.
4. Add lemon juice, salt and pepper.
5. Liquidise, and then add cream and at least 300ml/ ½ pint milk, or more, to your liking.

FRENCH ONION SOUP

(Serves 6)

This and the Minestrone soup are the two my husband makes, always with great enthusiasm and always complimented on.

Ingredients:

40g/1½ oz butter
40g/1½ oz onions, sliced thinly
900ml/1½ pints chicken stock
salt and pepper
bay leaf
French bread, sliced
sliced or grated cheddar cheese

Method:

1. Sauté onions in butter gently, until they start to turn brown.
2. Stir in stock, bay leaf, salt and pepper.
3. Bring to the boil, then simmer with lid on for 45 minutes.
4. Remove bay leaf.
5. Toast the slices of French bread under grill, then top with cheese and grill until melted.
6. Pop one into each bowl on top of soup (the bowls must be hot, an absolute necessity!).

MINESTRONE SOUP

(Serves 8)

Great for cold, dark days. A meal on its own.

Ingredients:

1 tbsp oil
25g/1oz butter
1 garlic clove, crushed
4 slices bacon, any kind, cut with scissors
2 carrots, finely sliced
1 leek, finely sliced
2 sticks celery, chopped
¼ cabbage, shredded
110g/4oz green beans or peas, tinned or fresh
1750ml/3 pints beef stock
2 tbsp tomato puree
salt and pepper
50g/2oz short macaroni
Parmesan cheese to serve

Method:

1. Heat oil and butter in large pan and sauté onion, garlic, bacon, carrots, leek and celery for 5 minutes.
2. Add remaining ingredients except macaroni.
3. Bring to boil and simmer with lid on for 45 minutes -1 hour.
4. Add uncooked macaroni in the last 15 minutes of cooking.
5. Serve in warm bowls with parmesan cheese.
   Freezes well.

CROUTÔNS

I always make my own. Very easy, cheaper and much nicer! Serve on the side with any soup.

Ingredients:

110g/4oz white bread, i.e. 3 slices, crust removed and cut into small cubes
2 tbsp olive oil

Method:

1. Preheat oven 180°C/Gas Mark 4.
2. Toss bread and oil together in a bowl until evenly coated.
3. Spread onto baking tray and cook for 10-15 minutes on a high shelf, until crisp and golden.
4. Cool and serve or keep air-tight for a few days, until required.

HAGGIS PARCELS WITH A WHISKY SAUCE

(Serves 4-6)
I saw this recipe years ago and remembered it because it is so easy, has a lovely flavour and very few ingredients.

Ingredients:

1 small good quality haggis
1 packet filo pastry
small carton double cream
about 1 tbsp grain mustard
about 1 tbsp whisky
fresh chives (optional)
melted butter

Method:

1. Follow instructions for filo pastry preparation - it is not difficult and great fun.
2. Cut out 4-6 squares with about 3 layers of pastry per square depending how many you are serving.
3. Place about 1 dessertspoon of haggis in the centre of pastry, leaving a good 2 inches of pastry all around. Gather the four corners into centre securing with melted butter which helps keep it all together.
4. Cook in pre heated oven, middle shelf, 190°C/Gas Mark 5 for 15-20 minutes. When cooked, if you want, tie a length of chive around neck of parcel.
5. Meanwhile place cream, grain mustard and whisky in a small pan and gently whisk to make sure the mustard is mixed through. Simmer for a couple of minutes.
6. Serve on warm plates, sauce first then place hot haggis parcel on top.

HAGGIS PANCAKES WITH FRUITY CHUTNEY AND SALAD LEAVES

(Serves 4-6)

Another one for the haggis lovers! I first had this in an Edinburgh restaurant and enjoyed it so much, I made my own version

Ingredients:

454g good quality haggis
Basic pancake mix:
110g/4oz plain flour
pinch salt
2 eggs
200ml/7floz milk
75ml/3floz water
2 tbsp melted butter
extra melted butter for cooking
fruity chutney, a bought one is fine
green salad leaves

Method:

1. First make the pancakes. Don't be put off, this is the most effort you will have to make for this lovely starter. The best bit is, it can be prepared ahead.
2. Sieve flour and salt in bowl.
3. Make a well in the middle and crack the two eggs in. Gradually add the milk and water using a hand whisk or electric hand whisk until all the flour is incorporated.
4. When ready to make pancakes add melted butter to batter, heat frying pan with a little butter then add about 2 tbsp of mixture, swirling to cover the base. The thinner the better.
5. After about half a minute, flip over and brown the other side. Slide onto a plate and continue to make pancakes, layering with greaseproof paper or foil.
6. When pancakes are completed divide haggis into sausage shapes of about the size of your finger. Place haggis in centre of pancake, turn in sides and roll up. Continue to make pancake parcels allowing one per person. Leave to the side until ready to serve.
7. To serve: heat haggis parcels in microwave for approximately 2 minutes. Remember to increase time if more than one pancake is being heated.
8. Place a handful of salad leaves on centre of plate, a dessert spoon of the fruity chutney on top then place the haggis parcel, which you have cut in half diagonally on top to finish. Serve immediately.

MAIN COURSES

PASTA CHICKEN BAKE

(Serves 8-10)

This was given to me by Lorna in 1996 and we have used it for large get togethers ever since.

Ingredients:

225g/8oz dried pasta shells
salt and pepper
225g/8oz onions
3 tbsp olive oil
2 garlic cloves
pinch saffron (optional)
1 level tbsp dried thyme
140ml/5floz dry white vermouth or white wine
2 x 400g/14oz cans chopped tomatoes
550g/1¼ lb passata
1 level tbsp caster sugar
700g/1½ lb skinless chicken breast fillets or boned chicken thighs
25g/1oz each butter and flour
425ml/15floz milk
200g/7oz full fat soft cheese
50g/2oz pitted black olives
5 level tbsp pesto sauce
basil sprigs to garnish

Method:

1. Cook pasta in boiling, salted water till just tender. Drain, run under cold water and set aside.

2. Roughly chop the onions. Heat 1 tbsp olive oil in a large saucepan, add onions, crushed garlic, saffron and thyme, then cook for 1-2 minutes. Pour in the dry vermouth and bubble for 2-3 minutes. Add the tomatoes, passata, seasoning and sugar. Bring to the boil and simmer for 15-20 minutes or until reduced by one third.

3. Cut the chicken into chunks. Place in a roasting tin. Drizzle over the remaining olive oil and season. Cover with foil and cook at 200°C/Gas Mark 6 for 10-15 minutes or until just cooked.

4. Melt the butter in a heavy-base saucepan and stir in the flour. Cook, stirring for 1 minute then gradually add the milk and whisk until smooth. Bring to the boil then simmer for a further 10-15 minutes, stirring occasionally. Remove from heat and whisk in the full-fat cheese; season.

5. Mix together the chicken, pasta, olives and tomato sauce and spoon into a 3.4L/6 pint dish with a depth of about 4cm/1½ inches. Lightly stir the pesto into the white sauce, to create a marbled effect. Spoon the white sauce over the chicken mixture.

6. Cook at 200°C/Gas Mark 6 for 30-35 minutes or until golden and hot through. Serve immediately garnished with basil sprigs.

To Freeze:

1. Cool, wrap and freeze at the end of step 5.

2. To use thaw overnight and cook as in step 6 for about 45-50 minutes.

CHICKEN NACHOS

(Serves 2)
An easy mid-week meal. Great served with 'Cowboy Caviar' (see recipe in *Miscellaneous* section) and sour cream and chive dip.

Ingredients:

2 chicken breasts, skinned
3 tbsp olive oil
1 large onion, finely chopped
3 cloves garlic, finely chopped
400g/14oz can chopped tomatoes
3 tbsp tomato purée
160g/5½ oz packet tortilla chips
100g/4oz Cheddar cheese, grated

Method:

1. Preheat oven to 200°C/Gas Mark 6.
2. Cook chicken breasts in oven for approximately 20 minutes, until juices run clear.
3. Allow to cool slightly.
4. Heat remaining oil in a large pan and add onion and garlic. Cook for 3-4 minutes until soft. Stir in tomatoes and purée.
5. Bring to boil, reduce heat and simmer for 15 minutes until rich and thick.
6. Shred the cooked chicken finely with 2 forks. Stir into the tomato sauce and season well.
7. Lightly oil a large, shallow ovenproof dish. Arrange tortilla chips over the base, spoon over sauce, sprinkle cheese over the top and bake for 10 minutes.

ITALIAN CHICKEN

(Serves 4)
A bit fiddly, but can be prepared ahead. Had it first for a rugby weekend in the 80's for family and friends. Serve with fresh tagliatelle.

Ingredients:

4 chicken breasts
flour and parmesan (enough to coat chicken)
1 egg
1 onion, sliced
1-2 cloves of garlic
2 courgettes, chopped
400g/14oz tomatoes, chopped
1 tbsp tomato purée
1 tsp basil
1 tsp oregano
4 slices of mozzarella

Method:

1. Coat the chicken in the egg and parmesan and fry until brown.
2. In the olive oil cook the onion and garlic for 5 minutes.
3. Add the tomatoes, courgettes, tomato purée, basil and oregano.
4. Place chicken in an ovenproof dish with sliced mozzarella on top. Cover with the sauce and a sprinkle of parmesan cheese. Cover dish and bake at 180-190°C/Gas Mark 4-5 for 20 minutes.
5. Take off cover 10 minutes before end.

SUN DRIED TOMATO CHICKEN

(Serves 4)

Easily prepared the night before. First had this at Moira's yet again. It has been passed around over and over.

Ingredients:

4 chicken breasts
juice of 2 lemons
2 tsp paprika
1 clove garlic
50g/2oz butter
12 sun dried tomatoes
300ml/½ pint double cream
salt and cayenne pepper
1 tbsp tarragon

Method:

1. Slice chicken into strips.
2. Mix lemon juice, paprika, garlic and tarragon.
3. Marinade the chicken in the mixture for at least an hour, though preferably overnight.
4. Melt butter, add chicken and cook for 10 minutes.
5. Cut tomatoes into four and add to the chicken.
6. Stir in the cream and boil for 2 minutes.
7. Cook in the oven 150-160°C/Gas Mark 2-3 for 30-45 minutes.
8. Serve with rice or roast potatoes.

CHICKEN VERONIQUE

(Serves 4)

A classic dish made with grapes and wine. This is put together with no particular quantities. Easy to adjust.

Ingredients:

4 chicken breasts
knob of butter
olive oil
plain flour
1 onion
1 garlic clove
white wine
green grapes
140ml/5floz double cream
salt and pepper

Method:

1. Heat oil and butter in frying pan. Coat chicken breasts in flour and brown. Place them in a casserole dish.
2. Soften onion and garlic in the pan, add in enough white wine and some green grapes, bubble and pour over the chicken to cover. Add salt and pepper.
3. Bake in oven at 180°C/Gas Mark 4 for 20-25 minutes.
4. Add cream and some more grapes and place back in the oven for another 5 minutes.
5. Serve with rice or cream potatoes and glazed carrots.

CHICKEN WITH BASIL AND MOZZARELLA

(Serves 6)

Yet again came from one of Moira's dinner parties. Lovely as always—and now used by lots of family and friends.

Ingredients:

6 chicken breasts with skin on
50g/2oz mozzarella cheese, sliced
3 tbsp fresh basil leaves, torn
a little chicken stock
6 thin slices smokey back bacon
3 tbsp sun dried tomato paste
300ml/½ pint single cream

Method:

1. Place cheese under the skin of the chicken, and then divide the basil leaves between the six breasts and place on top of the cheese.
2. Put into baking dish with about an inch of stock at the bottom. Place tin foil over the top and bake in the oven 180°C/Gas Mark 4 for 20 minutes.
3. Remove tin foil and place bacon around each chicken breast and place back in the oven for a further 20 minutes.
4. For the sauce, simply heat cream and tomato paste in a small saucepan until simmering.
5. When ready to serve use, place chicken in the centre of a heated plate and cover with sauce.

CHICKEN, CASHEW NUT AND PINEAPPLE

(Serves 4-6)

Taken from a Girl Guide Association recipe book in the 80's. Favourite family midweek dinner. A fussy child's favourite!

Ingredients:

1 cooked chicken, stripped
110g/4oz mushrooms
432g/15oz can pineapple rings, drained (juice kept for later) and diced
50-75g/2½ - 3oz packet cashew nuts
40g/1½ oz butter
2 onions

For the sauce:
2 chicken stock cubes
3 tbsp demerara sugar
2 tbsp soy sauce
juice from 432g/15oz can of pineapple
340ml/12 fl oz boiling water
2 tbsp vinegar
2 dessertspoons cornflour

See over for Method

Method:

1. Cut the chicken into bite sized pieces.
2. Prepare sauce – add approx 400ml/12floz boiling water to stock cubes, stir until dissolved. Add in rest of sauce ingredients EXCEPT CORNFLOUR. Allow to cool then gradually stir in the cornflour ensuring no lumps.
3. Add 40g/1½oz butter to large casserole pan over a low heat until melted. Chop onion into fairly large pieces and soften in butter (do not fry). Stir often to prevent sticking to base of pan.
4. When onion is soft, add sliced mushrooms.
5. Add in sauce mix and stir continuously until sauce thickens.
6. Next add cashew nuts and diced pineapple, continuing to stir.
7. Add diced chicken to mixture, allow time to heat through.
8. Serve with rice.

PORK WITH CAMEMBERT

(Serves 4)
Wonderfully easy. Serve with rice or potatoes. Dinner party material.

Ingredients:

450g/1lb pork fillet
1 tbsp of butter
3 tbsp of dry wine or dry cider
125-150ml/4-6 floz whipping cream
1 tbsp of chopped fresh mixed herbs
½ Camembert, peeled
1½ tsp Dijon mustard

Method:

1. Slice the pork into small medallions, beat between clingfilm.
2. Melt the butter and brown the pork. Cook the pork for 5 minutes and keep warm in oven.
3. Add the wine, cream and herbs to pan to collect sediment.
4. Finally add the cheese, stir gently until melted then add the mustard and more cream if needed, the sauce is now ready. Add pork.
5. Serve on warm plates.

LAKESHORE PORK - *AVOCA* VG

(Serves 6)
Simply delicious!

Ingredients:

1.3kg/3lb diced leg of pork, well trimmed (fillet is better)
seasoned flour (flour, salt, pepper, mustard powder and brown sugar)
olive oil
600ml/1 pint apple juice
300ml/ ½ pint chicken stock
2 tbsp Lakeshore mustard or wholegrain mustard
300ml/ ½ pint cream

Method:

1. Toss the pork in the seasoned flour and then brown it in some olive oil in small batches. Place in a flameproof casserole dish and cover with the apple juice and stock.
2. Add the mustard and bring to the boil, then transfer to an oven preheated to 180°C/Gas Mark 4 for 40 minutes.
3. Remove from oven, stir in cream and return to oven for 10 minutes.
4. If the sauce is a little thin, remove the meat and keep warm. Put the casserole over a moderate heat and simmer until the sauce is reduced and thickened. Return the meat to the pan.

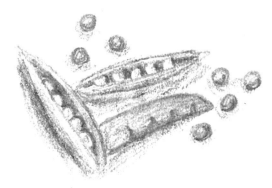

PORK WITH CIDER, MANGETOUT AND APPLE

(Serves 4)

Another easy dish. The only rush is getting everything out together on a hot plate. The family love it and it looks first class when plated.

Ingredients:

approximately 700g/1½ lb pork fillet
half a packet of mangetout, topped and tailed
1 apple, sliced
1 glass of cider
140ml/¼ pint single cream
50g/2oz butter
little oil
potatoes for four
grain mustard

Method:

1. Cut pork into medallions and fry in 25g/1oz butter and oil, keep warm in oven. Then add cider to pan to collect the sediment from the pork. Add cream and heat the sauce through.
2. In a small saucepan melt 25g/1oz butter and a little oil and stir-fry mangetout and apple slices. Keep to one side.
3. Boil potatoes and mash. Add approximately 1tbsp of grain mustard. Keep warm.
4. Place serving plates in the oven.
5. Now you are ready to put it all together. Put approximately 2tbsp of potato mash in the middle of the plate. Divide pork fillet between the plates and stack around the potato. Divide the apple and mangetout and place over the top, finishing off with the hot sauce. Serve immediately.

FRESH SALMON FILLET WITH TOMATO AND RED PEPPER

(Serves 4)

This recipe came on the packaging of the salmon; I have been using it ever since. Great served with new potatoes and a simple green salad.

Ingredients:

1 pack of 4 fresh salmon fillets
110g/4oz onions, chopped
15ml/1 tbsp olive oil
1 clove garlic, minced
15ml/1 tbsp tomato paste
140g/6oz red pepper
140g/6oz can chopped tomatoes
salt and pepper
1 tsp oregano, chopped
1 tsp parsley, chopped

For the bread topping:
50g/2oz bread slices, crusts removed
45g/3 tbsp parsley, chopped
½ garlic clove, minced
1 tbsp olive oil
salt

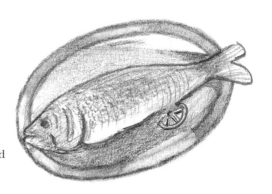

Method:

1. Preheat the oven to 190°C/Gas Mark 5.
2. Fry the onions in the olive oil until soft. Add the tomato paste, garlic, tinned tomatoes and herbs. Season and cook gently.
3. To roast a pepper – grill the pepper, keep turning until black. Cool in a polythene bag. When cool enough to handle, peel off the skin and remove the core and seeds.
4. Dice the red pepper and add to the mixture, heat the sauce thoroughly, stir in the chopped parsley, then leave to cool.
5. Place the bread into a food processor and make into fine breadcrumbs, add the chopped parsley and garlic and mix for a few more seconds, add the oil and salt, mix through.
6. Place the salmon into an ovenproof dish, season, then spread the sauce evenly over the top of the fillets. Sprinkle the breadcrumb mixture over the sauce.
7. Bake in the oven for 30-35 minutes.

SPECIAL FISH PIE

(Serves 6)

Special because the rice is at the bottom of the dish and the sauce has a wonderful colour and flavour from the spices used. It is very popular.

Ingredients:

225g/8oz long grain brown rice
600ml/1 pint boiling water
1 dessertspoon oil
½ onion, finely chopped
700g/1½ lb mixed seafood (I use salmon, any white fish, prawns and some smoked fish)
110g/4oz butter

110g/4oz mushrooms, sliced
75ml/3floz dry sherry
25g/1oz plain flour
1 tsp ginger powder
1 tsp hot curry powder
1 tsp mustard powder
300ml/ ½ pint single cream
110g/4oz Cheddar cheese, grated
cayenne pepper
salt and freshly milled black pepper

Method:

1. Pre-heat oven to 200°C/Gas Mark 6.
2. Heat the oil in a pan and add onion. Cook for 5 minutes then add the rice and stir.
3. Add the boiling water, stir and put the pan lid on and leave to cook over a very gentle heat for 40 minutes, or until all the liquid has been absorbed and the grains are tender.
4. Meanwhile melt 50g/2oz of the butter in a large frying pan and sauté the mushrooms for 2-3 minutes and then transfer into a dish.
5. Add a further 25g/1oz of butter to the pan and when it has melted add the uncooked fish with the sherry. Cook for 4-5 minutes over a medium heat then transfer to join the mushrooms, and prawns if using, in the dish. Pour the juices from the pan into a jug.
6. Melt the last 25g/1oz of butter to the pan, stir in the flour and add the ginger, curry powder and mustard. Stir until smooth.
7. Slowly stir in the reserved fish liquid and the cream and when thickened, gently add all the fish and mushrooms to the sauce and season. Put the rice in a buttered baking dish, spoon the fish mixture over and top with the grated cheese and a sprinkling of cayenne.
8. Put in a pre-heated oven at 200°C/Gas Mark 6 for 30 minutes.

BEEF AND GUINNESS CASSEROLE

(Serves 6-8)

Given to me by my sister, Julie. It was brought back from Canada: very Irish though. The kitchen smells wonderful while it cooks! Fabulous served with 'Braised Red Cabbage' and 'Mustard Mash' – recipes in *Salads and Vegetables* section.

Ingredients:

700g/1½lb braising steak, sliced
1 tbsp plain flour
1 tbsp oil
2 onions, sliced
225g/8oz carrot, sliced
2 sticks celery, sliced
225g/8oz ready to eat prunes
300ml/ ½ pt beef stock
300ml/ ½ pt Guinness
2 tbsp tomato purée
red pepper, chopped
salt and pepper

See over for Method

Method:

1. Heat oven to 160°C/Gas Mark 3.
2. Toss beef in flour.
3. Heat oil in pan and brown steak.
4. Add onion, carrot and celery.
5. Stir in prunes, stock, purée and Guinness, season and bring to the boil.
6. Bake for 1 hour 45 minutes.
7. Add pepper.
8. Cook for 15 minutes.
   Freezes well.

MEATY LOAF

(Serves 8)
Quick and easy and can be eaten warm with baked beans and potatoes.

Ingredients:

350g/12oz minced lamb
225g/8oz sausage meat
1 egg
1 large onion, finely chopped
1 tbsp brown sauce
1-2 tbsp freshly chopped parsley
salt and black pepper

Method:

1. Preheat oven to 180°C/Gas Mark 4.
2. Lightly grease a 500g/1 lb loaf tin.
3. Mix all the meat with egg, onion, brown sauce, chopped parsley and seasoning.
4. Pack mixture tightly into the greased loaf tin.
5. Cover tin with foil and bake for 50 minutes – 1 hour, until cooked.
6. Drain off any excess fat and leave in the tin to cool.

BEEF WITH ROOT VEGETABLES

(Serves 4-6)
Another recipe from a magazine and an easy mid- week family meal.

Ingredients:

1 tbsp oil
1 large onion, peeled and finely chopped
700g/1½ lb lean beef mince
1 tbsp plain flour
300ml/ ½ pint Guinness or stout
300ml/ ½ pint beef stock
2 tbsp Worcestershire sauce
2 tbsp tomato purée
1 bay leaf
450g/1lb potatoes, peeled and cut into small chunks
1 parsnip, peeled and cut into small chunks
½ swede, peeled and cut into small chunks
350g/12oz celeriac, peeled and cut into small chunks
4 tbsp olive oil

Method:

1. Heat oil in a large frying pan. Add onion and cook for 5 minutes, stirring occasionally, until soft. Add the beef mince and cook, stirring, for a further 5 minutes until browned all over.
2. Sprinkle in the flour and cook, stirring, for 1 minute. Remove from the heat and stir in the Guinness or stout, stock, Worcestershire sauce, tomato purée and bay leaf. Season with salt and freshly ground black pepper. Return to the heat, bring to the boil then simmer for 20 minutes.
3. Meanwhile, preheat the oven to 190°C/Gas Mark 5. Place the potatoes, parsnip, swede and celeriac in a large pan of water. Bring to the boil and par-boil for 5 minutes until just soft. Drain.
4. Spoon mince into a 2.3l/4 pint ovenproof dish. Pile the par-boiled vegetables on top. Brush with the olive oil and bake for 40 minutes until vegetables are tender and brown in places. Serve immediately.

MARZETTI
(Serves 4-6)
A strange name for a simple all in one dish. Great for large numbers.

Ingredients:

1 onion
450g/ 1 lb mince
110g/ ¼ lb mushrooms
75g/3oz grated cheese
pinch of herbs
1 small tin condensed tomato soup (295g)
1 small tin condensed mushroom soup (295g)
110g/4oz egg noodles or tagliatelle
seasoning
dash of sherry (optional)

Method:

1. Brown onion and mince, add mushrooms, seasonings, herbs and sherry.
2. Mix well and remove from the heat.
3. Cook noodles for 10 minutes.
4. Strain and add to mince with cheese and soups. Place in casserole.
5. Cover and cook for at least 1 hour at 150°C/Gas Mark 2.

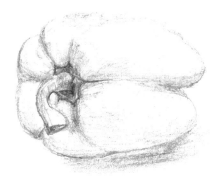

CUMBERLAND PIE

(Serves 6)

Another all in one dish. I love to prepare ahead especially for a family get together.
This is great served with 'Stir-fry Green Cabbage and Pine Nuts' – recipe in the *Salads and Vegetables* section.

Ingredients:

1 tbsp oil
1 large onion, peeled and finely chopped
700g/1½ lb lean minced beef
1 tbsp plain flour
2 tbsp Worcestershire sauce
1 tbsp tomato purée
390ml/13floz hot beef stock

For the topping:
450g/1lb carrots
625g/1lb 6oz swede
1.6kg/3½ lb potatoes
2 tbsp milk
50g/2oz butter
75g/3oz Cheddar cheese, grated
15g/ ½ oz fresh white breadcrumbs

Method:

1. Preheat the oven to 190°C/Gas Mark 5. Grease an ovenproof dish. Heat oil in a pan and add onion. Cook for 3-4 minutes then add mince. Cook for 5 minutes. Add flour and cook for a further minute. Add sauce, purée and stock. Simmer for 15 minutes until slightly thickened.
2. Meanwhile make the topping. Peel and roughly chop carrots and swede. Cook together in a pan of boiling salted water for 30 minutes until tender. At the same time, peel and roughly chop potatoes. Cook in a separate pan of boiling salted water for 25 minutes until tender.
3. Drain vegetables and return to pans. Add milk and half the butter to potatoes. Add remaining butter to carrots and swede. Mash the vegetables. Stir 50g/2oz cheese into the potatoes. Spoon the meat mixture into the ovenproof dish and spread the carrot mixture over the top.
4. Place potato over the top and fork it down to cover all the vegetables. Sprinkle with breadcrumbs and remaining cheese. Bake for 30-40 minutes until the cheese is melted and golden and the breadcrumbs are crisp.

IRISH STOVIES

Not really stovies as you may know, but a potato bake. Always made by my mum on request by our family friends, the Grays, when they visited us as children over the holidays. Quantities will vary on the number you are serving so I have just included the ingredients.

Ingredients:

potatoes
spring onions, chopped
tin of corned beef, broken into small pieces
basic cheese sauce (see recipe in 'Cheesey Sweet Potato & Cauliflower Bake')

Method:

1. Cook potatoes and slice when cool into thick slices. Line a gratin dish alternating with spring onion and corned beef.
2. Cover with cheese sauce.
3. Bake in oven 200°C/Gas Mark 6 for 30 minutes.

CHEESEY SWEET POTATO AND CAULIFLOWER BAKE

(Serves 6)

First had this at my friend Barbara's house at an informal supper. You can adjust quantities to suit numbers and tastes. This is my own version. I also use parsnip and/or ordinary potato to mix in with the sweet potatoes. Anything goes. Serve with a simple salad.

Ingredients:

2 large orange fleshed sweet potatoes, skins peeled
50g/2oz butter
50g/2oz plain flour
600ml/1 pint milk
225g/8oz cheddar cheese grated
1 small cauliflower, broken into large florets
3 tbsp snipped fresh chives
3 spring onions, chopped
4 slices bacon

Method:

1. Cut root vegetables into biggish chunks, leaving skin on ordinary potatoes if using, but peeling sweet potatoes. Toss in a little olive oil and roast in 200°C/Gas Mark 6 until cooked, about 40 minutes.
2. To make the sauce, put the butter, flour and milk into a small pan and whisk over a gentle heat until thickened, about 5 minutes. Season and stir in 50g/2oz cheese and chopped chives.
3. Cook the cauliflower in florets and when done add to the cooked vegetables in a roasting tin.
4. Grill the bacon and cut with scissors, then add to the cooked vegetables. Add spring onions and toss altogether. Put into an ovenproof dish and cover with sauce. Sprinkle on remaining cheese and bake at 200°C/Gas Mark 5 for 30 minutes.

ROASTED VEGETABLE MOUSSAKA

(Serves 8)

Experimented with this and used it for a family reunion as a vegetarian alternative – great success.

Ingredients:

1 medium onion, cut into strips
2 fennel bulbs, cut into strips
2 red peppers, deseeded and roughly sliced
1 medium aubergine, sliced
340g/12oz potatoes, peeled and sliced
5 whole garlic cloves
5 tbsp olive oil
Salt and pepper
400g/14oz can chopped tomatoes

4 whole pieces of sun dried tomato, chopped
225g/8oz tub cottage cheese
3 large eggs
175g/6oz Cheddar, grated
3 tbsp natural yogurt
thyme leaves to garnish

Method:

1. Put the vegetables and garlic in two roasting tins, drizzle with the oil and season. Cook at 220°C/Gas Mark 7 for 1 hour, tossing occasionally and swapping the tins around so the vegetables cook evenly and turn golden and soft.

2. Add the canned tomatoes and the sun dried tomato to the vegetables, then mix well to continue. Return the vegetables to the oven to cook for a further 10-15 minutes.

3. In a bowl, beat together the cottage cheese, eggs, Cheddar cheese and yogurt, then season. Spoon the vegetable mixture into a shallow 1.8-2.3L/3½ – 4 pint ovenproof dish, then spread the cheese mixture over the top.

4. Cook at 200°C/Gas Mark 6 for 20-30 minutes or until the moussaka is golden and bubbling. Garnish with thyme leaves to serve.

To Freeze:

1. Complete the recipe to the end of step 3, cooling the vegetable mixture before spooning the cheese mixture on top. Freeze.

2. To use, thaw overnight. Complete the recipe. Cover the moussaka with foil after 20 minutes if the top starts to turn too brown, then continue to cook for a further 20 minutes until it's hot to the centre.

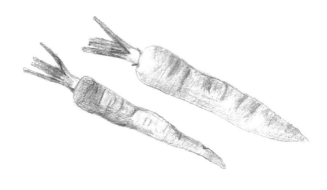

SALADS & VEGETABLES

GREEN PEA SALAD

(Serves 4)

Had this first in Brighton in 1997 at another family reunion. Made by Saskia, my second cousin, whom we all adore. This is great with a cold dressed salmon.

Ingredients:

340g/12oz frozen petit pois
50g/2oz stuffed green olives
50g/2oz candied peel
lots of garlic (2/3 cloves)
1-2 inches of fresh root ginger peeled and finely chopped
2 tbsp lemon juice
7 tbsp sunflower oil
1 heaped tsp paprika
salt
parsley or mint finely chopped

Method:

1. Fry garlic, oil, paprika and ginger briefly.
2. Add peel, peas, olives, lemon juice and salt and pepper, stir till peas are defrosted.
3. Serve cold with parsley or mint sprinkled on the top.

CARROT AND COURGETTE SALAD - *AVOCA*

(Serves 8)

A little bit different from traditional coleslaw, with a lovely nutty orangey taste.

Ingredients:

5 carrots, peeled and coarsely grated
5 courgettes, coarsely grated
a bunch of fresh coriander, chopped (reserve a sprig for garnish)
4 tbsp French dressing
1 dessertspoon roasted pumpkin seeds
1 dessertspoon poppy seeds
juice of 1 orange
grated zest of 2 oranges

Method:

1. Put the grated carrots and courgettes in a bowl and mix with the coriander, French dressing, seeds, orange juice and most of the grated zest.
2. Garnish with the remaining orange zest and a sprig of coriander.

BULGAR WHEAT SALAD

(Serves 6-8)
A lovely change from rice salad, especially if you like the aroma and taste of mint.

Ingredients:

200g/7oz bulgar wheat
1 tsp salt
340ml/12floz boiling water
450g/1lb tomatoes, chopped
½ cucumber, diced

Dressing:
60ml/2floz oil
60ml/2floz lemon juice
2 tbsp fresh mint, finely chopped
1-2 cloves garlic
6 tbsp chopped parsley

Method:

1. Mix salt and wheat, add water and leave for 15-20 minutes.
2. Mix dressing ingredients all together and stir into wheat. Leave in fridge overnight.
3. To serve, add tomatoes and cucumber to bulgar wheat.

CHICKEN AND WATERCRESS SALAD

(Serves 4-6)
A lovely salad, given to me by my friend, Janie, in the 80's.

Ingredients:

50g/2oz almonds
bunch of watercress
large celery (hearts and leaves)
450g/1lb cooked chicken
juice of ½ orange
Approx 300ml/½ pt mayonnaise

Method:

1. Toast the almonds.
2. Beat the juice of the orange into the mayonnaise.
3. Chop the watercress, celery and chicken.
4. Mix together.

CORONATION CHICKEN

(Serves 6)
What can I say?
This is the recipe I have used and used all my married life. Originally from the cream book in the 70s, my most popular and most requested dish.

Ingredients:

3 tbsp freshly whipped cream
110g/4oz onions, finely chopped
1 tbsp oil
1 level dessertspoon curry powder
140ml/ ¼ pint stock
2 level tsp tomato purée
juice of ½ a lemon
4 level tbsp apricot jam
140ml/ ¼ pint real mayonnaise
140ml/ ¼ pint salad cream
450g/1 lb cooked chicken, chopped

Method:

1. Fry the onions in the oil till soft, add curry powder and cook for 1 minute.
2. Stir in the stock, tomato purée, lemon juice and apricot jam. Bring slowly to the boil, simmer 10 minutes and cool.
3. Stir the mayonnaise, salad cream and the cream together. Now add the cooled tomato mixture and chicken and mix well.
4. Season to taste with salt and pepper.

Good served with a salad of rice, currants, red pepper, diced cucumber and garnished with watercress.

SPINACH, SUN DRIED TOMATO, PARMESAN, PINE NUTS AND PASTA SALAD - *AVOCA*

(Serves 8)
Pasta salad can become a little bit boring so this one makes an interesting and tasty change.

Ingredients:

500g/1lb 2oz pasta (penne or fusilli)
4 tbsp freshly grated Parmesan cheese
2 tbsp pine nuts, toasted
3 tbsp roughly chopped sun dried tomatoes with their oil
125ml/4floz extra virgin olive oil
175g/6oz baby spinach leaves, shredded

Method:

1. Cook the pasta in boiling salted water until tender, then drain.
2. Add all remaining ingredients except the spinach, mix well and season to taste.
3. Leave to cool, and then add the spinach.

ORIENTAL COLESLAW
This was served at the street party on 4th July in Denver, while on holiday – Yummy!

Ingredients:
1 whole cabbage, shredded
$\frac{1}{2}$ cup slivered almonds
$\frac{1}{4}$ cup butter
$\frac{1}{4}$ cup rice wine vinegar
2 tbsp soy sauce
$\frac{1}{4}$ tsp pepper
6 spring onions, chopped
$\frac{1}{2}$ cup sunflower seeds
$\frac{1}{2}$ cup oil (vegetable or sesame seed)
$\frac{1}{2}$ cup sugar
$\frac{1}{2}$ tsp salt
1 pkt dry egg noodles, crushed (do not cook)

Method:
1. Combine chopped cabbage and chopped spring onions in a ziplock bag and store in fridge overnight (minimum 2 hours).
2. Brown almonds and sunflower seeds in butter. Allow to cool.
3. Add crushed egg noodles to the mixture.
4. For the dressing, combine oil, vinegar, sugar, soy sauce, salt and pepper.
5. Combine all ingredients in a large bowl and serve.

MANDARIN SALAD
My sister Nikki's favourite. American.

Ingredients:
$\frac{1}{2}$ cup sliced almonds
3 tbsp sugar
$\frac{1}{2}$ head iceberg lettuce
$\frac{1}{2}$ head romaine lettuce
1 cup chopped celery
2 whole spring onions, chopped
300g/11oz can mandarin oranges

Dressing:
$\frac{1}{2}$ tsp salt
$\frac{1}{4}$ cup vegetable oil
1 tbsp chopped parsley
2 tbsp sugar
2 tbsp vinegar
dash of Tabasco sauce

Method:
1. In a small pan, over medium heat, cook almonds and sugar stirring constantly until almonds are coated and sugar dissolved. Watch carefully as they will burn easily.
2. Cool and store in airtight container.
3. Mix all dressing ingredients and chill.
4. Mix lettuces, celery and onion.
5. Just before serving add almonds and mandarins.
6. Toss with dressing.

MUSTARD MASH

Great with all meat dishes.

Ingredients:

potatoes
grain mustard
a little butter and milk

Method:

1. Boil potatoes and mash with butter and milk.
2. Add approximately 1 tbsp of grain mustard.

GLAZED CARROTS

No particular recipe here, my girls just wanted this included!

Ingredients:

carrots, cut into sticks
knob of butter
1 tsp sugar
mixed herbs
salt and pepper

Method:

1. Cover carrots, barely, with boiling water and cook for 5 minutes.
2. Drain, add butter, sugar, herbs and salt and pepper. Cook for a further 5 minutes, stirring, being careful not to over cook.

STIR-FRY GREEN CABBAGE AND PINE NUTS

(Serves 4)

Had something similar to this in a seafood restaurant in Anstruther, with close friends, Philippa and Andrew, who are also great gourmets. This is my own version.

Ingredients:

1 sweet heart cabbage, shredded
couple of slices of bacon, chopped small with scissors
1 tbsp pine nuts, optional toasted
½ onion, sliced
olive oil
salt and black pepper

Method:

1. Heat oil and soften onion and bacon.
2. Add cabbage and stir-fry, mixing well, for 5 minutes.
3. Add pine nuts, salt and black pepper and serve.

ROAST PARSNIPS AND APPLE

(Serves 4)
Came from Lorna, yet again. Just that little bit different and very tasty.

Ingredients:

900g/2lb even-sized parsnips
700g/1½ lb old potatoes
2 crisp tart eating apples
3 tbsp oil
25g/1oz butter
2 level tbsp chopped chives

Method:
1. Peel vegetables, cut into chunks. Peel, core and chop the apples. Cook together in boiling water for 3 minutes. Drain well.
2. Heat oil and butter. Add vegetables and apples and stir well until well coated.
3. Roast at 220°C/Gas Mark 7 for 45 minutes till very tender.
4. Serve with chives and seasoning.

BRAISED RED CABBAGE

(Serves 8)
This is my family's favourite vegetable. Great served with any casserole, and turkey at Christmas.

Ingredients:

2 tbsp sunflower oil
1 tsp ground coriander
½ tsp cinnamon
¼ tsp freshly grated nutmeg
2 large onions, thinly sliced
900g/2 lb red cabbage, finely shredded
2 tbsp soft dark brown sugar
4 tbsp red wine vinegar
salt and black pepper
2 tbsp redcurrant jelly - optional

Method:
1. Heat the oil in a large, heavy based pan. Add the spices and stir-fry for 1 minute.
2. Add the onion and cabbage and stir-fry for 2 minutes.
3. Stir in the sugar and vinegar with salt and pepper, cover and cook over a very low heat for 45 minutes – 1 hour, stirring frequently.
4. Add the redcurrant jelly, mix well and cook for a further 5 minutes.

Linda McDonald has generously shared her recipes in this very personal cookbook to raise much needed funds for the mothers and babies who need treatment in Malawi.

As a midwife at the Royal Infirmary of Edinburgh, she is familiar with all the needs of a new mother and child. The midwives at the Bottom Hospital in Lilongwe, Malawi need our help to provide education, equipment and transportation for pregnant mothers to get them safely to the hospital.

Thanks to the Royal Bank of Scotland's sponsorship, Linda's book can make a real difference in its contribution. All of us can help by buying the book and have some fun trying out the recipes at home.

Sarah Brown, *President of Piggy Bank Kids.*

DESSERTS

RASPBERRY AND CINNAMON TORTE

(Serves 8)
A simple but delicious dessert.

Ingredients:

150g/5oz unsalted butter, softened
150g/5oz caster sugar
150g/5oz ground almonds
2 tsp vanilla extract
150g/5oz self-raising flour
1 large egg, beaten
2 tsp ground cinnamon
225g/8oz raspberries or blackberries
icing sugar to dust
cream to serve

Method:

1. Preheat the oven to 190°C/Gas Mark 5. Grease a 23cm/9 inch springform cake tin, and line with greased greaseproof paper.
2. Place the butter, sugar, ground almonds, vanilla extract, flour, egg and ground cinnamon in a large bowl and beat together with a wooden spoon until smooth and blended. Alternatively use an electric whisk.
3. Spread half this mixture into the tin and flatten lightly with your hand. (It's important to work quickly to prevent the raising agent in the flour from being activated before baking.) The quicker you are, the lighter the torte will be. Sprinkle the fruit over the mixture.
4. Using your fingers, gently dot and spread the remaining almond mixture over the berries, leaving some still showing. Bake for 1 hour until golden on top and crumbly to the touch. Cover with foil if it starts to brown too quickly. Allow to cool slightly, remove from the tin, dust with icing sugar and serve torte with cream.

WHITE CHOCOLATE AND BAILEYS TORTE

(Serves 8 – 10)
Had this first at Stobo Castle on an occasional but always enjoyable visit. I asked the cook, Teresa, for the recipe. She, as always, was very obliging.

Ingredients:

175-280g/6–10oz chocolate digestives
75-110g/3–4oz butter
340g/12oz white chocolate
500ml/18floz double cream
4 tbsp Baileys
2 tbsp Jamieson Whiskey

Method:

1. Whizz biscuits in blender.
2. Melt butter in saucepan and add to biscuits and mix. Spread the mixture evenly in a tin with a removable base and put in fridge to chill.
3. Melt the chocolate in a microwave, checking and stirring 30 seconds at a time to make sure that it doesn't burn.
4. Whip the cream until it makes soft peaks.

5. Warm the Baileys and Jamieson in microwave for 30 seconds – make sure it is warm and not hot. Add to chocolate mixture, stir and fold (it may look like it will separate but it shouldn't)
6. Add the Baileys and chocolate mixture to the whipped cream and fold.
7. Spread the mixture evenly on top of the biscuit base and leave in fridge for approx 6 hours.

BAKEWELL TART
(Serves 8)

Delicious and looks great. Worth making your own pastry and doing the lattice work in the right size tin. Very rewarding to make.

Ingredients:

For pastry:
300g/10oz plain flour
150g/5oz butter or margarine, chilled and cubed
2 tbsp caster sugar
1 medium egg, beaten with 1 tbsp water

For filling and decoration:
110g/4oz butter, softened
110g/4oz caster sugar
2 medium eggs, lightly beaten
25g/1oz self-raising flour
75g/3oz ground almonds
½ tsp almond essence
6-8 tbsp raspberry jam
2 tbsp flaked almonds
beaten egg to glaze
whipped cream or custard to serve

Method:

1. Lightly grease a 23cm/9 inch round, 3cm/1¼ inch deep, fluted, loose-based flan tin.
2. To make the pastry, sift the flour into a bowl, add the butter and, using your fingertips, rub in until the mixture resembles fine breadcrumbs. Stir in the sugar then make a well in the centre. Add the beaten egg and use a round-bladed knife to bring the mixture together to form a firm dough. Wrap in cling film and chill for 30 minutes.
3. On a surface lightly dusted with flour, roll out two-thirds of the chilled pastry to a 28cm/11inch circle. Place the pastry over a rolling pin and carefully lift it over the prepared tin. Press the pastry into the base and sides of the tin then trim the edge by running the rolling pin over the top. Add all the pastry trimmings to the remaining pastry and chill, together with the lined tin, for 20 minutes.
4. To make the sponge filling, place the butter and the sugar in a large bowl. Using an electric whisk or a wooden spoon, beat the butter and sugar together until the consistency is smooth and creamy and the mixture is pale in colour. Gradually add the eggs, beating well after each addition, until they are thoroughly incorporated. Sift the flour over the creamed mixture and fold in with the ground almonds and almond essence.

5. Spoon the jam into the pastry case and, using the back of a spoon, spread it in an even layer. Carefully spread almond filling over jam, again levelling with the spoon. Take care not to leave gaps around the edges as jam can leak while cooking. Preheat oven to 180°C/Gas Mark 4 and place a baking sheet inside. On a lightly floured surface, roll out remaining pastry to a 25 x 12.5cm/10 x 5 inch rectangle. Cut into 9–10 strips, each about 12mm/ ½ inch wide.

6. Arrange pastry strips in a lattice pattern – place one straight across the filling at one end of tin then place another at a right angle to the first, in the opposite direction. Repeat until all strips are used. Decorate with flaked almonds then glaze pastry with the beaten egg. Bake on preheated baking sheet for 35-45 minutes until the sponge filling is well risen, golden and springy to the touch. Cool slightly. Serve warm with whipped cream or custard.

APPLE TART

(Serves 8)

This came from the same old recipe book in the 70's and is made frequently. It is my husband's favourite – you can't beat it.

Ingredients:

550g/1¼ lb cooking apples, peeled, cored, and sliced
75g/3oz plus 1 tbsp caster sugar
225g/8oz self raising flour
175g/6oz butter or margarine
1 egg, separated
1 tbsp milk
2 tbsp apricot jam
50g/2oz ground almonds

Method:

1. Place the apples and the sugar in a saucepan and simmer gently until pulpy. Cool.
2. Place the flour in a bowl, rub in the butter, and then mix to a firm dough with the egg yolk and milk. Wrap in cling film and chill.
3. Roll out a generous half of the pastry and use to line a 20cm/8 inch loose bottom sandwich tin.
4. Spread the base with the apricot jam.
5. Sprinkle half the almonds over the jam, then the apples, finishing with the remaining almonds.
6. Top with the reserved pastry, seal the edges well and cut a couple of slits in the top of the pastry.
7. Brush the pastry with beaten egg white and sprinkle with a little sugar.
8. Bake in a preheated oven 200°C/Gas Mark 6 for about 30 minutes until golden brown.
9. Serve warm with cream or ice cream.

EASY CHEESECAKE

(Serves 6-8)

First had this at one of Debbie's many dinner parties. Now known as "Debbie's Cheesecake". I have used it over and over again; the only difference is I use Marks and Spencer's Summer Fruit Compote which is delicious. However you can use a fruit pie filling if you prefer.

Ingredients:

175g/6oz digestive biscuits, crushed
75g/3oz butter
300ml/10floz double cream
110g/4oz sieved icing sugar
300g/10oz Philadelphia cheese
fruit compote to serve

Method:

1. Melt butter, add the crushed digestive biscuits, mix well.
2. Line a 20cm/8 inch tin with removable base with mixture, chill.
3. Hand beat cheese and sieved icing sugar together until smooth. Softly whip cream and fold into cheese mixture until everything is well combined. Put on top of digestive base and level flat. Chill until required.
4. Turn out and pour over fruit compote, serve.

RASPBERRY TRIFLE

(Serves 6-8)

Absolutely *NO* jelly and definitely worth making your own custard. Freeze the egg whites for a future date or use to make pavlova.

Ingredients:

6 trifle sponges
200g/7oz raspberries, fresh or frozen
2 tbsp raspberry jam
1–2 tbsp sherry
300ml/½ pint double cream
custard (see below)
toasted flaked almonds – to decorate

Method:

1. Split sponges in half and spread with jam on one side, sandwich together and cut into 6.
2. Place in glass dish. Sprinkle with sherry, then fresh raspberries or frozen and allow to defrost.
3. Make custard (see below). Pour over. Cool in fridge. Cover with cream and sprinkle over the almonds.

CUSTARD:

Ingredients:

600ml/1 pint milk
4 egg yolks
4 tbsp caster sugar
2 tbsp cornflour
few drops vanilla essence

See over for Method

Method:

1. Using a fork, whisk yolks, cornflour and sugar in a bowl to combine.
2. Add a little milk to mix.
3. Warm remaining milk adding egg mixture, stirring all the time.
4. Bring slowly to boil, keep stirring to avoid lumps until thick.
5. Cool slightly, add vanilla and pour over raspberries.

LEMON ROULADE

(Serves 8)

Found this recipe in a magazine last year and have made it many times since. It is lovely and lemony, just how I like it.

Ingredients:

5 medium egg whites
150g/5oz caster sugar
1 tsp cornflour
300ml/ ½ pint double cream
12 tbsp homemade lemon curd (recipe below)
icing sugar, for dusting

Lemon curd can be made 2-3 weeks ahead and kept in the fridge.

110g/4oz butter cut into small chunks
250g/9oz caster sugar
finely grated rind and strained juice 2 large unwaxed lemons
3 medium eggs, beaten

Method for lemon curd:

1. Put butter, sugar, lemon rind and juice into a pan, and heat gently until butter and sugar have dissolved, stirring constantly.
2. Remove from heat and allow to cool.
3. Whisk beaten eggs into mixture. Return pan to a very low heat and cook for 10-15 minutes, stirring constantly, until thick enough to coat the back of a spoon. Do not boil.
4. Pour lemon curd into sterile jars and put a waxed paper disc on top of each.
5. Leave to cool and keep in fridge until ready to use.

Method for roulade:

1. Preheat oven to 150°C/Gas Mark 2. Line a Swiss roll tin with non-stick baking parchment.
2. Whisk egg whites until stiff, using an electric whisk. Add half the sugar and whisk until mixture is stiff and shiny. Add remaining sugar with cornflour and whisk thoroughly.
3. Spoon meringue mixture into tin and level surface. Bake for 45 minutes until firm to the touch. Leave to cool in tin for 1 hour then turn out onto a sheet of baking parchment and peel away paper backing.
4. For the filling, whip cream to soft peaks and mix in 4 tablespoons of lemon curd. Spread remaining 8 tablespoons (I use less) of lemon curd over meringue, leaving a narrow border around the edge. Spread cream over lemon curd.
5. Roll meringue up from one of the short ends, then put on a plate with join facing downwards. Chill until needed. Dust with icing sugar to serve.

PAVLOVA

(Serves 8)

This has to be number one in this section. I have made hundreds over the years and it never fails to impress. I took orders for Edinburgh University years ago, and my husband became a dab hand at creating them, when I was working. It came from an old recipe book in the 70s.

Ingredients:

4 egg whites
225g/8oz caster sugar
1 tsp vanilla essence
1 tsp vinegar
2 tsp cornflour
425ml/15floz double or whipping cream
raspberries, or a mixture of strawberries, black grapes and kiwi fruit, or banana and crushed Flake

Method:

1. Mark a 23cm/9 inch circle on a sheet of silicone paper and place on a baking tray.
2. Whisk the egg whites in a large bowl or mixer until stiff.
3. Continue whisking adding the sugar a tablespoon at a time until the mixture is thick and glossy and all the sugar is used up.
4. Fold in the vanilla essence, vinegar and cornflour and spoon the mixture inside the circle to give a neat shape. Make a slight well in the centre with the sides slightly higher.
5. Cook in preheated oven 150°C/Gas Mark 2 for 1 hour.
6. Cool slightly, then turn out onto your hand peeling off the paper and carefully place on a serving plate.
7. Decorate with softly whipped cream and fruit.

PROFITEROLES

(Serves 4)

Not difficult – lovely with fudge sauce which has firmed up in the fridge.

Ingredients:

50g/2oz butter or margarine
65g/2½ oz plain flour, sieved
2 eggs, beaten
150ml/¼ pint cold water

Method:

1. Preheat the oven to 220°C/Gas Mark 7. Put the fat in a pan with 150ml/¼ pint cold water and heat until melted. Bring to the boil, then add the flour all at once and mix well.
2. Remove pan from the heat and beat well until smooth and glossy, and mixture leaves side of pan.
3. Place pastry mixture in a large bowl and cool for 10 minutes. Gradually whisk in eggs, a little at a time, until mixture forms a stiff dropping consistency.
4. Using a teaspoon, spoon 16 small heaps of mixture on to two dampened baking sheets, spacing them about 5cm/2 inches apart.
5. Cook the pastry in the oven for 20-25 minutes or until golden brown and crisp. Using a small sharp knife, make a slit in the side of each cooked choux bun to release the steam, then transfer the buns to a wire rack and leave to cool completely.
6. Fill with whipped cream and pour over fudge sauce.

FUDGE SAUCE

Delicious. Serve with ice cream or, as I use it, over profiteroles for a change.

Ingredients:

150ml/ ¼ pint double cream
110g/4oz butter
110g/4oz soft brown sugar

Method:

1. Put everything into a pan and stir over a gentle heat.
2. Once the butter has melted and the sugar dissolved, boil fast for 5 minutes.
3. Keep warm until you are ready to serve. It keeps in the fridge for several days.

TOBLERONE MOUSSE

(Serves 4)
A Pilates shared recipe. Again easy and great served in wine glasses.

Ingredients:

200g/7oz Toblerone
6 tbsp boiling water
300ml/ ½ pint double cream, whipped
2 egg whites, stiffly beaten
chocolate or Toblerone, grated, to serve

Method:

1. Place Toblerone with the 6 tablespoons boiling water in a bowl over a pan of boiling water.
2. Once melted, allow to cool until nearly set.
3. Fold in the whipped cream and then the egg whites.
4. This can be used as a filling for pavlova or put in small glasses and served with grated chocolate or Toblerone on top.

CRUNCHIE PUD

(Serves 4)
We all love this one, especially my daughters who make it for their friends. Easy!

Ingredients:

1 egg white
300ml/8floz double or whipping cream
4 Crunchie bars

Method:

1. Bash Crunchies in their packets carefully with a rolling pin.
2. Whisk egg white until stiff then whip the cream until stiff.
3. Fold the egg white into the cream.
4. Stir in the crushed Crunchies.
5. Spoon into four wine glasses and chill.

BAKING

BROWN BREAD

My grandmother's recipe. Traditional Irish loaf. I have been making it for years.

Ingredients:

3 breakfast cups of self raising flour
1½ cups of soft bran flakes (not always easy to get)
½ cup wheatgerm
3 tsp sugar
large tsp baking soda
level tsp salt
Approximately 600ml/1 pint milk

Method:

1. Line a loaf tin with silicone paper.
2. Mix all dry ingredients together in a bowl, combine with milk to make a porridge like consistency.
3. Put in tin and bake 200°C/Gas Mark 6 for 45 minutes until the loaf sounds hollow when tapped and skewer comes out dry when tested.

SODA BREAD

Best eaten on the day it's made. Memories of childhood.

Ingredients:

450g/1lb plain flour
1 level tsp bicarbonate of soda
1 tsp caster sugar
½ tsp salt
about 400ml/14fl oz buttermilk

Method:

1. Mix all the dry ingredients together in a large bowl. Gradually mix in the buttermilk to give a moist dough.
2. Place in a greased 900g/2lb loaf tin and bake in an oven preheated to 230°C/Gas Mark 8 for 30 minutes, until the loaf sounds hollow when tapped and skewer comes out dry when tested.
3. Place on a wire rack to cool.

SCONES

My famous scones. The only secret here, which my mother told me, was to hardly roll and to make five with a medium size round cutter. I have also found that placing the scones in a circle touching each other on the baking tray, helps them to rise evenly. I have two recipes here, one with an egg and one without. It is not easy to tell the difference.

SCONES 1

Ingredients:

225g/8oz self raising flour
50g/2oz margarine
pinch salt
1½ tbsp caster sugar
1 egg, beaten
milk or buttermilk to bind

Method:

1. Rub margarine into flour until it resembles breadcrumbs. Mix in sugar and salt.
2. Add egg and enough milk to create a soft doughy texture, not too moist.
3. Roll out on floured surface and cut five or six scones depending on the size of cutter. I sometimes rub a little milk over surface of scone to help browning.
4. Place on floured baking tray and bake in preheated oven 200°C/Gas Mark 6 second shelf from the top, for 10-15 minutes until browned on top.

SCONES 2

Ingredients:

225g/8oz self raising flour
pinch salt
40g/1½ oz margarine
1½ tbsp caster sugar
300ml/½ pint milk

Method:

1. As above, but omitting the egg and using 300ml/½ pint milk instead.

SWEET SCONE

Easy to make and a change from the traditional scone.

Ingredients:

150g/5oz self raising flour
50g/2oz margarine
75g/3oz caster sugar
1 egg and milk to bind

Method:

1. Rub margarine into flour, add sugar.
2. Make into soft dough with egg and enough milk to bind.
3. Line a 18cm/7 inch tin with silicone paper and spread mixture evenly to cover evenly in tin.
4. Sprinkle with some caster sugar and bake in preheated oven 190°C/Gas Mark 5 for 20 minutes.

MERINGUES

(Serves 6-8)
These are easy to make if you don't cut corners and a great dessert to make weeks ahead.

Ingredients:

3 egg whites
175g/6oz caster sugar

See over for Method.

Method:

1. Place egg whites in a clean bowl and whisk until very stiff using an electric whisk.
2. Add 1 tablespoon of sugar at a time while still whisking, after 1 minute add another until all the sugar is used up remembering to allow 1 minute whisking in between each addition.
3. Put a piece of silicone non-stick baking parchment on a baking tray and either pipe or spoon meringues to whatever size you want. I usually use a soup spoon.
4. Place in oven on lowest shelf at lowest number for 2-3 hours, to dry out.
5. Turn oven off and leave until cool.

CARROT CAKE

Or should I say Chrissie's carrot cake? I have yet to taste one better.

Ingredients:

110g/4oz grated carrots
227g (undrained weight) can crushed pineapple
50g/2oz chopped walnuts
175g/6oz plain flour
175g/6oz of sugar
1tsp baking powder
¾ tsp bicarbonate of soda
½ tsp cinnamon
½ tsp salt
200ml/7floz cooking oil
2 eggs

For topping:
75g/3oz Philadelphia cheese
75g/3oz softened butter
½ tsp vanilla
175g/6oz icing sugar, sieved

Method:

1. Mix all dry ingredients together.
2. Beat eggs and oil separately and add in to dry ingredients, mixing well.
3. Add in walnuts, pineapple and carrots.
4. Line an 20cm/8 inch tin with silicone paper and put mixture in, smoothing the top.
5. Bake in the oven 180°C/Gas Mark 4 for 1 hour.
6. Make topping – cream the cheese, butter and vanilla together and gradually add icing sugar. Cover top of cake when cold.

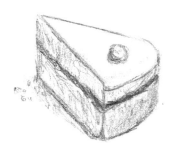

CHOCOLATE FUDGE CAKE

The ultimate chocolate cake for special occasions.

Ingredients:

50g/2oz cocoa powder
175g/6oz unsalted butter
290g/10oz caster sugar
3 eggs beaten
250g/9oz plain flour
1½ tsp bicarbonate of soda
½ tsp baking powder

Icing:
75g/3oz unsalted butter
4 tbsp milk
340g/12oz icing sugar
2 tbsp cocoa powder

Filling:
75g/3oz unsalted butter
175g/6oz icing sugar, sifted

Method:

1. Preheat the oven to 180°C/Gas Mark 4.
2. Grease two 20cm/8 inch round sponge tins at least 4cm/11/2 inch deep and line base with greaseproof paper.
3. Blend the cocoa with 240ml/8floz boiling water.
4. Soften butter and place in a bowl with sugar and 4 tablespoons of chocolate mixture, beat until light and fluffy.
5. Gradually beat in the eggs and remaining chocolate mixture.
6. Sift the flour, bicarbonate of soda and baking powder and gently fold in.
7. Divide the mixture between the cake tins. Bake for 25 minutes until risen and firm to the touch. Leave in tins for 5 minutes then turn out on to a wire tray to cool completely.
8. Meanwhile, for the icing, place butter and milk in a small pan and heat gently until melted. Sift in icing sugar and cocoa and beat until smooth. Reserve 4 tablespoons of the icing and chill the rest until thickened, stirring occasionally.
9. For the filling, beat the butter and icing sugar until smooth then beat in the reserved chocolate icing. Chill until firm.
10. To assemble the cake, remove lining paper and sandwich the sponges with the chocolate butter cream filling and spread the icing over the top and sides with a palette knife.

CHOCOLATE SPONGE SLICES

This recipe came from Ruth ten years ago and is still popular. It is easy to make and cut into slices.

Ingredients:

1½ tbsp cocoa blended with 3 tbsp boiling water and 2 tbsp of milk
125g/4½ oz margarine
125g/4½ oz caster sugar

3 eggs, beaten together
150g/5oz self raising flour
1½ tsp baking powder

Icing:
60g/2½ oz margarine
1 tbsp cocoa
250g/9oz sieved icing sugar
3 tbsp hot milk
1 tsp vanilla essence

Method:

1. Cream margarine and sugar, add eggs, flour and cocoa mixture and beat until well combined.
2. Line a small Swiss roll size tin with silicone paper and put mixture in, spreading it out evenly.
3. Bake in oven 180°C/Gas Mark 4 for 20 minutes. Cool in tin.
4. Make icing. Melt margarine, blending in cocoa, then stir in icing sugar, hot milk and vanilla essence.
5. Beat until smooth and thick. I find leaving it in the fridge to firm helps spreading.
6. When cake is cold cover with icing and cut into fingers.

ORANGE CAKE

This is a favourite of our friends, Phillipa and Andrew. Usually made for their birthdays and special occasions. Recipe came from my grandmother.

Ingredients:

150g/5oz self raising flour
75g/3oz margarine
1 level tsp baking powder
125g/4½ oz caster sugar
pinch of salt
2 eggs
1 tbsp milk
1 orange, grated and squeezed

For icing:
150g/5oz icing sugar, sieved
75g/3oz margarine
orange juice from ingredients

Method:

1. Sieve all dry ingredients, add margarine, sugar, eggs, orange rind and 1 tbsp milk.
2. Beat well and divide between two 18cm/7 inch tins lined with silicone paper.
3. Bake in oven 180°C/Gas Mark 4 for 20 minutes.
4. To make icing – cream sugar and margarine together with as much orange juice as needed to give the right consistency. Be careful not to use too much orange juice, add it a teaspoon at a time. Use icing to fill and top cake.

CHOCOLATE BROWNIES

The best brownies I have ever tasted.

Ingredients:

200g/7oz dark chocolate
200g/7oz unsalted butter at room temperature
200g/7oz caster sugar
2 large eggs and 2 yolks
2 tbsp vanilla essence
110g/4oz flour
4 tbsp cocoa powder
1/2 tsp baking powder
1/2 tsp salt

Method:

1. Pre-heat oven to 160°C/Gas Mark 3.
2. Melt chocolate.
3. Cream butter and sugar until fluffy.
4. Add eggs and vanilla until creamy.
5. Beat in flour, cocoa powder, baking powder, salt and melted chocolate.
6. Spoon into lined tin.
7. Bake for 40 minutes, till risen and spongy.

COFFEE OATMEAL BISCUITS

My mum's recipe.

Ingredients:

110g/4oz margarine
110g/4oz plain flour
110g/4oz porridge oats
50g/2oz caster sugar
1 level tsp baking powder
2 dessertspoons Camp coffee essence
walnuts, chopped to decorate

For icing:
75g/3oz margarine
150g/5oz icing sugar, sieved
2 dessertspoons Camp coffee essence

Method:

1. Cream margarine and sugar, add coffee essence.
2. Stir in remaining ingredients bringing them altogether in one ball.
3. Roll out on a floured surface until about 1cm/1/2 inch thick then cut out circles using cutters about 10cm/4 inch size.
4. Place on greased baking tray and bake in oven 180°C/Gas Mark 4 for 20 minutes.
5. Cool on wire tray and make icing.
6. Beat all icing ingredients together and use to sandwich biscuits together .
7. Decorate top with walnuts.

EASY SHORTBREAD

First had this at Lorna's house, when our children were babies.

Ingredients:

110g/4oz self raising flour
110g/4oz plain flour
110g/4oz cornflour
110g/4oz caster sugar
225g/8oz butter

Method:

1. Sieve all dry ingredients together.
2. Melt butter and add to dry ingredients.
3. Pat into tray bake size tin, sprinkle with a little sugar and bake in oven 150-160°C/Gas Mark 2-3 for 50 minutes.
4. Cool in tin and cut before completely cold.

RUM TRUFFLES

Delicious. Recipe is very old and came from a friend's grandmother.

Ingredients:

4 egg yolks
225g/8oz cooking chocolate
110g/4oz unsalted butter
175g/6oz icing sugar
2 dessertspoons rum

Method:

1. Cream butter and sugar.
2. Beat in eggs yolks.
3. Melt chocolate.
4. Mix all ingredients together (chocolate last as it sets quite quickly).
5. Cool in fridge and roll into balls (using sprinkles to coat if desired).

TIFFIN

Best ever.

Ingredients:

25 digestive biscuits
4 tbsp cocoa powder
4 tbsp coconut
4 tbsp drinking chocolate
110g/4 oz margarine
397g tin condensed milk

Method:

1. Melt margarine and mix all ingredients together.
2. Either form small balls and roll in coconut or cocoa or spread in tray and cut when firm.

MALTESER SLICE

This is the ultimate chocolate hit! The recipe came from Helen, a friend at work. We all know it and love it!

Ingredients:

110g/4oz butter
3 tbsp golden syrup
250g/9oz Dairy Milk chocolate plus 350g/12oz for the top
225g/8oz digestive biscuits, crushed
225g/8oz Maltesers, halved

Method:

1. Melt the butter, chocolate and syrup in heavy pan.
2. Add the biscuits and Maltesers. Press into baking tray.
3. Melt the chocolate carefully and spread evenly over the top.
4. Chill and slice when nearly set.

This book is part of the national effort to change lives in a part of Africa that has been friends with Scotland for a long, long time.

The challenges facing Malawi are enormous, but Scots can, and are, making a difference. Thank you for your donation. It will make a big difference to the renewal of Bottom Hospital.

Jack McConnell MSP, *First Minister of Scotland*

MISCELLANEOUS

FRENCH DRESSING - *AVOCA*

Why buy, when you can make this lovely dressing which lasts ages in the fridge?

Ingredients:

300ml/ ½ pint sunflower oil
300ml/ ½ pint olive oil
300ml/ ½ pint peanut oil
300ml/ ½ pint red wine vinegar
salt and pepper
2 garlic cloves
3 tbsp grainy mustard
2 dessertspoons honey

Method:

1. Place all the ingredients in a bowl and liquidise.
2. This can be stored in a bottle and shaken vigorously before using.
3. It will keep in the fridge for several weeks.

COWBOY CAVIAR

I had this first on the 4th July while visiting my sister in Denver, Colorado, at a street party. Very 'more-ish'.

Ingredients:

2 tbsp red wine vinegar
1 tbsp Tabasco
1½ tsp vegetable oil
1 clove garlic, minced
⅛ tsp black pepper
1–2 avocados, cubed
425g/15oz can black beans, washed and drained
325g/11oz can sweetcorn, drained
⅔ cup spring onion
⅔ cup coriander
225g/8oz chopped tomatoes
½ tsp salt

Method:

1. Mix vinegar, Tabasco, oil, garlic and pepper in large bowl.
2. Add remaining ingredients to vinegar mixture.
3. Serve with tortilla chips.

SALSA DIANE

This recipe came from my friend Lorna's Canadian friend. Iain makes it every year with his tomatoes from the greenhouse.

Ingredients:

8 cups peeled chopped tomatoes
1 cup roasted chopped sweet peppers
3 cups chopped onions
1 cup vinegar
150g/5oz can tomato paste
3 cloves garlic
1–2 tsp dried crushed chillies
1 tbsp salt
½ tsp pepper
coriander

Method:

1. Mix all ingredients thoroughly in a large pan.
2. Boil till soft: 1½ –2 hours.
3. Jar and lid immediately.

GIN AND TONIC SORBET

This was given out at my Pilates class, a great place for exchanging recipes and information. This recipe is for fun. I use it at Christmas or at dinner parties in between courses to clear the palate. Serve in liqueur or sherry glasses.

Ingredients:

150ml/5floz tonic
2 tbsp lemon juice
1 tbsp lime juice
3 tbsp sugar
2 tbsp gin

Method:

1. Put all ingredients into a pan and stir over a low heat until the sugar is dissolved. Churn until frozen or freeze until nearly solid then mash with a fork and return to freezer.

N.B. depending how you like your G & T: replace lemon juice with more lime (or vice versa) and double the gin.

RASPBERRY JAM

I make this every year and give half away. You can't beat homemade jam.
Just remember 1lb of raspberries gives 1lb of jam. Raspberries have their own pectin so the jam sets easily, which is why it's the easiest jam to make.

Ingredients:

1.8kg/4lb raspberries
1.8kg/4lb sugar

Method:

1. Boil raspberries in their own juice for 1 hour.
2. Add sugar and bring to the boil. Continue to boil rapidly for 15-20 minutes stirring all the time.
3. Meanwhile have a saucer in the fridge to test the jam. When the time is up, take the pan off the heat and place a little of the jam on the saucer which is cold, and check it wrinkles when you push it with your finger from the side. If it wrinkles it is ready; if not, boil for another couple of minutes and test again.
4. Warm clean jam jars in the oven to sterilise and pour jam in using a jug to avoid a mess.
5. Cover the jam with discs of waxed paper and place lid on tightly.

THREE FRUITS MARMALADE

I like this marmalade because it has no rind. My mum's recipe. The cup I use measures 8floz.

Ingredients:

1 orange, quartered and rind left on
1 lemon, quartered and rind left on
1 grapefruit, quartered and rind left on
1.8kg/4lb sugar
9 cups water

Method:

1. Liquidise chopped fruits with 3 cups of the water.
2. Soak overnight in remaining water.
3. Simmer for 1 hour.
4. Add sugar and boil for approximately 25 minutes stirring all the time.
6. Meanwhile have a saucer in the fridge to test the marmalade. When the time is up, take the pan off the heat and place a little of the marmalade on the saucer which is cold, and check it wrinkles when you push it with your finger from the side. If it wrinkles it is ready; if not, boil for another couple of minutes and test again.
7. Warm clean jam jars in the oven to sterilise and pour marmalade in using a jug to avoid a mess.
8. Cover the marmalade with discs of waxed paper and place lid on tightly.

LEMON AND APRICOT MARMALADE

Delicious – now been passed down through three generations of Lorna's family.

Ingredients:

450g/1 lb lemons
340g/ ¾ lb dried apricots
1750ml/3 pints water
1.35kg/3 lb sugar

Method:

1. Wash lemons, squeeze juice and tie pips in muslin. Mince or chop peel and pith.
2. Place in a large bowl, add water and leave for 24 hours.
3. Put in a pan and simmer for 1½ hours.
4. Remove pips, add sugar and chopped apricots, bring to boil stirring all the time. Boil until setting point is reached.
5. Meanwhile have a saucer in the fridge to test the marmalade. When you think setting point is reached, take the pan off the heat and place a little of the marmalade on the saucer which is cold, and check it wrinkles when you push it with your finger from the side. If it wrinkles it is ready; if not, boil for another couple of minutes and test again.
6. Warm clean jam jars in the oven to sterilise and pour marmalade in using a jug to avoid a mess.
7. Cover the marmalade with discs of waxed paper and place lid on tightly.
8. Makes approx. 5 pounds.

This summer my family and Linda's both had the privilege of hosting 3 delightful African children and a leader from the African Children's Choir through our church. Their infectious energy and love of life was a joy to hear.

Linda seeks the support of others to assist underprivileged Mums in Malawi, whose children are less fortunate than our healthy, talented young visitors, and whose babies often have no chance of surviving.

In old Scottish communities, sharing was a way of life, right down to cups of sugar. Let's get that concept back. I am delighted to endorse this exciting venture and hope you will ensure its goal of supporting work at Bottom Hospital. In buying this special recipe book, you will make a difference.

Sandra Brown, *Scotswoman of the Year, 2005*

INDEX

INDEX